THE WORLD OF
HORSES

Jackie Budd

KINGFISHER
BOSTON

KINGFISHER
a Houghton Mifflin Company imprint
222 Berkeley Street
Boston, Massachusetts 02116
www.houghtonmifflinbooks.com

First published in 2004

10 9 8 7 6 5 4 3 2
2TR/0704/TIMS/PICA/128 MA

Copyright © Kingfisher Publications Plc 2004

LIBRARY OF CONGRESS CATALOGING-IN-PUBLICATION DATA
Budd. Jackie.
    World of Horses/Jackie Budd—1st ed.
    p. cm.
    Includes index.
Contents: All about horses—
Going riding—In the past—
Horses today—Reference
section. 1. Horses—
Juvenile literature.
2 Horse breeds—
Juvenile literature.
[1. Horses.
2. Horsemanship.]
I. Title.
SF302.B8424 2004
636—dc22
        2003061908

ISBN 0-7534-5753-9

Printed in China

Series editor: Camilla Hallinan
Design: Ben White and John Jamieson
Cover design: Anthony Cutting
Picture research: Elaine Willis

First published as
Horses

CONTENTS

ALL ABOUT HORSES

The story of the horse begins way back at the dawn of time, millions of years before the first people appeared on Earth. It is a story full of adventure and drama which starts with a struggle simply to stay alive.

Running wild

Although there are hardly any true wild horses left today, there are still many horses living in a wild state. Most of these, such as the mustang of North America and the Australian brumby, are actually "feral" horses which were once domesticated but escaped to live and breed in the wild. The Camargue ponies of southern France roam free but are all owned by people.

▼ Over millions of years, differences in environment and climate slowly changed the horse. However, since people began to tame, use, and breed horses about 3,500 years ago, it has been the human race that has had the greatest influence on the horse story.

There are still many unanswered questions in our knowledge of how horses evolved. However, by using fossils and other scientific evidence, experts have been able to piece together a fascinating picture of how early horses spread across the world to become the many shapes and sizes of horse we know today.

As the Earth's climate changed, species of animal appeared and disappeared, with only the fittest and the most adaptable clinging to existence. By the time people had begun to tame and ride the horse, nature had already created one of the toughest and most talented survivors in the animal kingdom.

Evolution of the horse

Hyracotherium, originally called *Eohippus* or Dawn Horse, was the ancestor of the modern horse. It was 10 inches (25 cm) tall and had four toes on each foot.

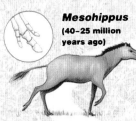

Hyracotherium (55–40 million years ago)

Mesohippus and *Mery-chippus* were larger than *Eohippus*. They had longer legs and three toes on each foot instead of four.

Mesohippus (40–25 million years ago)

Gradually, the Earth's dense, wet forests became firm, grassy plains. To avoid extinction, the early horses changed too.

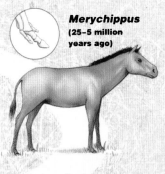

Merychippus (25–5 million years ago)

Pliohippus (5–2 million years ago)

Pliohippus had large, flat grinding teeth for feeding on grass, and longer, stronger legs supported by hooves.

By the end of the last ice age, millions of wild horses that we could recognize roamed Europe and Asia—the species *Equus caballus*.

Equus caballus (1.5 million years ago)

The horse family

All animals that have a single-toed hoof on the end of each leg belong to the horse family—the genus (group) we call *Equus*. This makes it easy to spot the relatives of the horse, which include zebras, donkeys, asses, and mules. But how did horses as unlike each other as the Shetland and the Shire, the Arabian and the ass, develop into such different creatures when they shared a common ancestor?

Horse homeland
America was the birthplace of the horse—the only place where fossils of *Eohippus* have been found. Over millions of years, until the last ice age separated America from the rest of the world, herds of horses migrated across land bridges to Asia and beyond.

Mighty mustangs

Although the first horses evolved in America, for some reason they became extinct there before the last ice age. It was not until Spanish adventurers brought their spirited mounts to the New World that horses returned to the American continent. Some horses escaped or were stolen by Native Americans. These became the ancestors of the mustang (1).

Asses, zebras, and donkeys

The earliest and most primitive horses to migrate from America millions of years ago were the ancestors of today's zebras and asses.

The domestic donkey (8) is descended from the African ass.

KEY
1 Mustang
2 Camargue pony
3 Brumby
4 African wild ass
5 Kiang (Tibetan wild ass)
6 Indian onager
7 Common zebra
8 Domestic donkey
9 Przewalski's horse
10 Shire
11 Arabian
12 Akhal-Teke
13 Exmoor pony
14 Shetland pony
15 Falabella

Today, there are over 200 breeds of horse and pony. The smallest is the Falabella (15), which was originally bred in Argentina. It stands just 34 inches (80 cm) tall.

These animals began moving when the climate was still tropical. As it cooled, they wandered south into the Middle East, Asia, and Africa. Today there are three races of wild ass—the African (4), the kiang (5), and the onager (6)—and there are three kinds of striped zebra —the common zebra (7), Grevy's zebra, and the mountain zebra.

Only one truly wild horse is left today. It is called Przewalski's horse (9), after the Russian explorer who rediscovered it on the remote Mongolian steppes in 1870.

Hot and cold

Two broad groups of horse developed from the migrating primitive herds —the northern "cold bloods" and the southern "hot bloods."

Heavy horses

Cold-blooded horses include the huge Shire (10). The ancestors of this gentle giant migrated into the cool marsh and forest lands of northern Europe after the last ice age. With few natural enemies to escape from, these horses grew tall, heavy, and slow. Their bulky bodies helped them to survive the cold, and extra bones in the spine gave more room for the digestive organs. Huge feet spread the horse's weight on the soft, muddy ground and hairy "feathers" kept the legs warm.

EUROPE

ASIA

AFRICA

AUSTRALIA

Feral horses include mustangs (1), Camargue ponies (2), and brumbies (3).

What makes a mule?

Despite being different species, asses and horses can be bred together to create new animals like the mule (from a donkey stallion and horse mare) and the hinny (from a donkey mare and horse stallion). The offspring are very strong and tough, but they are always infertile so they can never produce their own young.

Pony power

A smaller type of horse also spread across Europe and Asia—the pony. It became a specialist at surviving all kinds of harsh climates and conditions. Hardy native British breeds, such as the Exmoor (13) and Shetland (14), grew thick coats and long manes and tails to help them survive the cold.

Fiery horses

The Arabian (11), the oldest and purest horse breed, is a hot-blood. Arabians became lean and athletic, with dish-shaped heads adapted to breathing in dry, dusty air and fine hair to cope with the desert heat. Other fast breeds include the Akhal-Teke (12) of Asia.

Danger!

Long before people arrived on the scene, evolution taught horses how to survive. The success of the species depended on avoiding becoming dinner for a passing predator. Therefore, every herd member was constantly on the lookout for danger, ready either to escape as fast as possible or, if necessary, to turn and fight.

▼ On the open African grasslands, young zebras can be an easy catch for a hungry lion.

Horse sense

 Everyone knows at least one rule about being near horses—don't stand behind one or you may get kicked! This isn't because all horses are bad tempered. It's simply easy to forget that despite the fact that they have been domesticated, horses are still wild animals at heart, and almost every horse and pony follows the same basic instincts as the wildest mustang.

Fight or flight?

As with any hunted animal, fear is a horse's strongest emotion. When a horse feels threatened, it will panic and react in one of two ways—fight or flight. Because a horse is built for speed, its first instinct is to run from danger. However, if cornered or forced to face an attacker, it is well equipped to kick and bite to defend itself. Bucking is a natural defense reaction, too. That's why young horses may buck when first saddled up.

Who's boss?

Fighting between horses is quite rare, even in the wild, because living together and keeping the peace is essential to herd life. However, a stallion may fight to ward off a threat from a rival. In a field, horses and ponies have their own "pecking order" too, with bites and kicks sorting out who's boss.

Making friends with a pony and teaching it to trust you means taking time to learn about and understand what makes it behave the way it does. Ponies are naturally wary and can be easily startled, shying at any sudden, unexpected movement, mainly because its ancestors' attackers often sprang without warning. So always be calm and sensible near a pony, talking and running your hand firmly over its body to let it know where you are.

Grooming

Touch is used between horses to communicate, and they often groom each other by nibbling on one another's necks and backs.

▶ Horses have their own special body language and facial expressions. If you watch closely, you will soon pick up clues about what a favorite horse or pony is thinking and feeling.

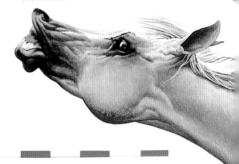

alert

angry

afraid

content

flehmen*

*smelling or tasting something interesting!

9

Body talk

The overall shape and appearance of a horse or pony is called its conformation. Looking at this shape is one way in which people compare horses. The parts of the horse's body are called the points. Learning to recognize these points is useful, as you will hear them talked about at your riding school or by a vet.

What makes a good horse?

Look at the ponies in a nearby field or at your riding school. Few have a perfect conformation. Some features of "poor" conformation are to do with being unattractive or out of proportion, such as having a too-large head. Others can indicate a physical weakness and are more serious.

Muscle-bound

This amazing drawing of a horse's muscles is from *The Anatomy of the Horse* by George Stubbs (1724–1806). Stubbs was the first artist to study a horse's body in detail. As a result, his drawings and paintings were very realistic.

Poll · Crest · Mane · Neck · Withe[rs]
Forelock · Eye · Nostril · Cheek · Elbo[w] · Forearm · He[el]
Ears · Muzzle · Shoulder · Stifle · Belly · Knee · Chest · Cannon bone · Hoof

Hands high

Horses are measured from the ground to the withers, and their height is given in "hands"—a measurement of 4 inches (10.2 cm), which is actually based on the width of a man's hand. The exceptions are Shetland ponies and miniature horses, which are measured in inches.

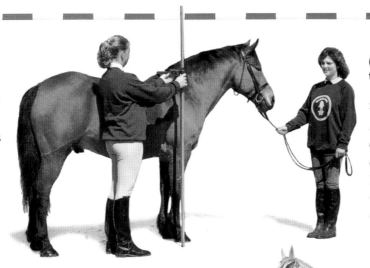

◄ A small horse 14.2 hh (hands high) or less is termed a pony.

Skeleton

A horse's skeleton gives clues about its breed. For example, a carthorse will have thick, heavy bones to support its weight, whereas a racehorse will have long, fine bones.

Back

Loins

Croup

Dock

Tail

Quarters

Flank

Thigh

Hock

Fetlock

Coronet

Pastern

Bony framework

At first glance, a horse's skeleton looks very different from ours, but take a closer look. There are more similarities than you would think!

HUMAN	HORSE
1 finger/ toenail	1 hoof
2 wrist	2 knee
3 elbow	3 elbow
4 heel	4 hock
5 knee	5 stifle

Horses and ponies come in all shapes and sizes. Although each breed has its own characteristics, all horses are built in much the same way. Even after thousands of years of living with people, horses are still designed to gallop fast to escape predators and have the stamina to keep up with a moving herd.

Walk

The paces

Paces, or gaits, are the different ways a horse moves. By using different gaits, a horse can increase or decrease its speed and still remain in balance. We have two gaits—walking and running. With only two legs, the sequence of our footfalls remains the same but is quickened. Having twice as many ④ legs as we do, horses, not surprisingly, have more gaits.

The jump

Although horses rarely need to leap obstacles in the wild, jumping comes naturally because the action is just like an extra-big canter stride.

The walk

This is the slowest pace, in which you can clearly hear the hoofbeats come down in an even "one-two-three-four" sequence. The horse starts with one hindleg, then the foreleg on the same side, then the opposite hindleg, then that foreleg. There are always at least two feet on the ground at any time.

The trot

This is a horse's most natural pace, in which it springs from one diagonal pair of legs to the other, with a moment in between when all four feet are off the ground. ③

A true jump has five stages:
(1) Approach—the horse steadies and dips its head to get the jump in focus.
(2) Take-off—it brings its quarters underneath and lifts its shoulders and forelegs.

Gallop

Trot

The canter

In the canter, there are three distinct beats. First one hindfoot, then the other hindfoot with its opposite forefoot, then the other forefoot striking out on its own (the "leading leg"), and finally a moment of silence when all four feet are off the ground.

The gallop

This is the fastest and most exciting pace. The gallop is basically a canter with extra speed and longer strides. When the horse gallops, its hindlegs push it forward with greater power. Racehorses can gallop at speeds of up to 45 mph (72 km/h)!

There are four gaits that come naturally to the horse—the walk, trot, canter, and gallop—and each gait has its own particular pattern of hoofbeats. Some horses also have specialized gaits which they have been trained to do or which are in their breeding.

②

①

(3) Flight—the horse rounds its back and stretches out to clear the fence.
(4) Landing—the forelegs straighten out, then touch down.

As the hindlegs land, the horse lifts its front end, then strides away.

Canter

Colors and markings

①

②

③

There are so many different colors and markings that every horse and pony you see is unique. This is helpful when it comes to recognizing or describing a particular one. But why are there so many colors? For the answer, we have to go back in time again, to look at the horse's ancestors.

Wall eye

Blaze

▲ Horses usually have deep brown eyes, but you may sometimes see a wall eye—a white or white-blue eye.

Sock

Pastern

④

⑤

⑥

⑦

⑧

⑨

⑩

▼▶ White hairs often come in small patches on the head and the lower legs. A horse or pony with no markings is sometimes called whole-colored.

White face

Stripe

Star

Snip

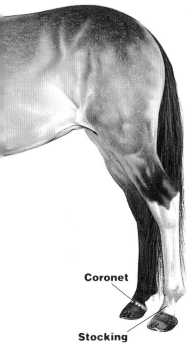

Coronet

Stocking

▲ Leg markings are often described according to the area they cover, such as a white heel, or white fetlock.

⑪

Mix and match

What makes a chestnut, a bay, or a dapple gray? It's all to do with the color of the coat's individual hairs. Each hair either has a pigment (coloring) or it does not. Hairs without pigment are white. Those with pigment are red or black. The mixture of white, red, and black in the coat, and the shade of the red hairs, give us all the horse colors we can see.

KEY
1 **Chestnut—mixture of red and black**
2 **Appaloosa—dark spots on white coat**
3 **Fleabitten gray—flecks of black or brown on white**
4 **Palomino—pale chestnut with white mane and tail**
5 **Black—all black**
6 **Dun—sandy brown with black mane and tail**
7 **Piebald—large irregular black-and-white patches**
8 **Bay—reddish brown with black mane and tail**
9 **Dapple gray—mottle effect of white and black**
10 **Brown—dark red and black**
11 **Strawberry roan—white hairs sprinkled through chestnut**

Over the ages, horses' coats became camouflaged so that they blended in with their surroundings—whether it was sand, rock, scrub, or a grassy plain—and with the rest of the herd. The harder it was for their enemies to see them, especially at the dangerous hours of dusk, the greater their chance of survival.

Painted ponies
People have always prized certain distinctive coat colors. For example, Native Americans liked "colored" horses with dramatic piebald or skewbald (white spots on a color other than black) markings. When they rode into battle, they often painted their ponies with special marks, too, to bring good luck.

▼ This painting by Amos Bad Heart Bull, an Oglala Sioux from Pine Ridge Reservation, shows Crazy Horse and Sitting Bull mounted before warriors at the battle of the Little Bighorn in 1876.

1 Neat stables

Look for a tidy stable area and tack room, with clean, roomy stables in good condition.

2 Happy horses

Make sure ponies look content, well-fed, and alert. Check that their feet are in good condition and they have no sore spots.

3 Muck heap

The muck heap should be neat and tucked away from the stables, and should be cleaned **regularly**.

5 Safety first

Tools must be put away carefully, and first aid and fire equipment must be close at hand. No smoking is a strict rule in stable areas.

4 Friendly welcome

A well-run school will have polite and cheerful staff who will be happy to help you.

GOING RIDING

A riding school is where most people first meet horses and ponies close-up. Schools can be large, busy stables or small places with only a few ponies. Whatever the size, it is important to choose a good riding school so that you can learn to ride properly. A well-run school will have horses suitable for beginners and qualified instructors to make riding safe and fun.

6 In gear

All the riders should be wearing safety helmets. A good school will have up-to-date helmets that you can borrow or rent.

7 Class lessons

Check that there are no more than six riders in a group—so you'll have lots of help and plenty of space.

8 Under cover

Does the school have an indoor area? It may be handy in wet or wintry weather.

The lunge

This young rider is having a lesson on the lunge. The instructor controls the pony using a long rein called the lunging rein. This means the rider can concentrate on her position and balance. These lessons are a good way of building up a beginner's confidence.

Ask local horse experts, such as a blacksmith or farrier, a saddler, or a pony club secretary, which riding school they can recommend. Schools approved by recognized riding organizations will guarantee high standards. Once you have found the right one, arrange a lesson—happy riding!

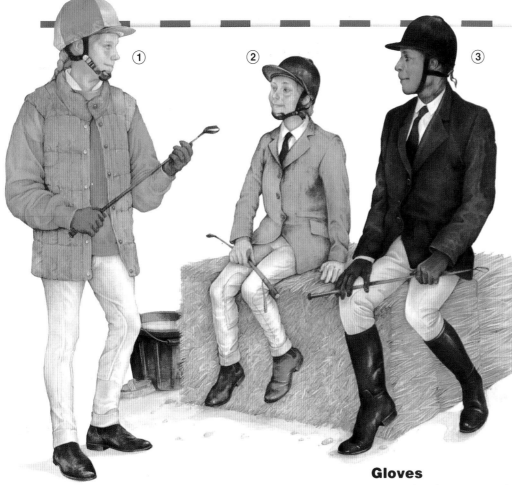

① ② ③

1 Casual gear

For casual riding you can wear a jockey skull type of safety helmet. The one here is shown with a silk peaked cover. Choose a loose-fitting top with long sleeves if it is cool. Wrap up warm in cold weather and wear a raincoat when it's wet.

2 Games

If you take part in pony club games or a small show, you'll need a skull cap with a dark velvet cover, a white or pale shirt with a club tie or plain dark one, a tweed jacket, and light-colored jodhpurs.

Riding gear

When you're riding, you must wear gear that is safe, comfortable, and practical. If you go to a show or to another important event, you have to get fitted out correctly. However, when you first start riding, it's not essential to have lots of expensive clothing. What's most important is that you have sensible footwear with a low heel and a well-fitting riding hat which is up to the latest approved standards.

Gloves

Frozen hands won't work well, and sweaty ones slip on the reins, so always wear gloves—wool ones in winter, thin cotton ones in summer, and leather ones at shows.

Jodhpurs

Jodhpurs or riding breeches are the most comfortable for English riding; jeans are best for open-country riding. Jodhpurs are made of stretchy fabric with knee panels to prevent saddle rubs.

Boots

Short jodhpur boots with a low heel are ideal for young riders. Long boots can be leather or rubber, but must fit closely to your legs.

Body protector — **Skull cap** — ④

3 At a show

Appearing at a larger show means a slightly different look. Wear a skull cap with a dark velvet cover or a hard hat with a fixed peak. Most riders wear either a black or a navy jacket, jodhpurs or breeches—short "jods" which end just below the knee—and long boots.

4 Cross-country

Safety comes first when riding cross-country. Hats must be top-quality skull caps. A body protector is also essential. Its padded jacket fits under or over a sweater, and it may have shoulder pieces.

Air space — **Padding** — **Lining** — **Chin strap**

Choosing a hat*

Your hard hat or safety helmet must:
- have thick, all-over inside padding
- be snug, but not tight, and sit level
- allow two fingers underneath at the back
- cover your temples, your forehead, and the back of your head
- stay in place when you bend over, even when unfastened.

When wearing your hat, remember always to do the chin strap up tightly.

In the past, riding gear was not as safe and sensible as it is today. Imagine galloping over fields and hedges dressed up like the 18th-century woman shown on the right! In the 1700s and 1800s, most wealthy women rode sidesaddle —they perched with one leg looped over the hook of a special saddle, which was designed so that both legs rested on the same side of the horse. They sometimes wore a riding habit, including a hat with a veil and a long, heavy skirt.

Sitting pretty

Today, a few brave riders keep the sidesaddle tradition alive, and side-saddle classes are popular at shows in Britain.

▶ **Riding habit from the late 1700s**

*When choosing a hat, look for the American Society of Testing and Materials (A.S.T.M.) label. These labels are usually stuck to the top inside the hat and are awarded only if the hat meets tough safety standards.

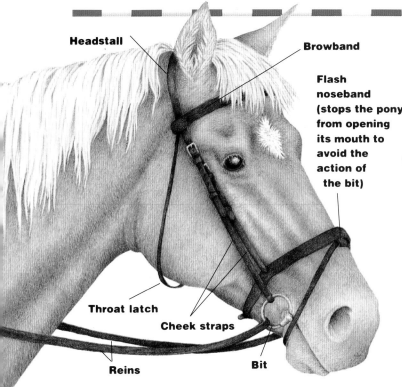

Headstall

Browband

Flash noseband (stops the pony from opening its mouth to avoid the action of the bit)

Throat latch

Cheek straps

Reins

Bit

Bridles and bits

Tack, or saddlery, is the name given to all the equipment a horse or pony wears when it is ridden. There are many different pieces of tack, and each piece has a special use, but the two main items that every pony wears are a saddle and a bridle. Both are usually made of leather and must fit well to be comfortable and effective.

The bridle is basically a set of straps that fasten around the pony's head and support the bit in its mouth. The reins attached to the bit are your communication lines to the pony.

Bits

There are many kinds of bit, and each type works in a slightly different way. Most quiet ponies wear a simple snaffle bit. Stronger ponies may need a curb bit with a curb chain, such as a Pelham. A double bridle is used by skilled riders and well-trained horses for very finely-tuned control.

▲ **Snaffle—a straight bar, or one with a single or double joint in the center.**

▲ **Pelham—usually has two reins but many have one if a bit converter is used.**

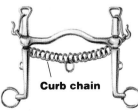

Curb chain

▲ **Double—has two bits, a thin bridoon (snaffle), and a curb (such as this Weymouth). Each bit has its own rein, and only one rein is used at a time.**

Pelham bridle

Double bridle

Cavesson noseband

Bit converter

Putting on a bridle

1 Facing forward, stand close to the pony's near (left) side and put the reins over its head. Hold the bridle so the bit is in front of the mouth, and guide in the bit with your left hand. You may need to slip your thumb into the side of the gums where there are no teeth to encourage the pony to open up its mouth.

2 Gently bring the headstall up over the ears, one by one. Then pull out the forelock and tidy the mane. Check that the bit is at a comfortable height. It should just wrinkle the pony's lips so that it looks like it's smiling. Make sure that the bit is not too high and tight or too low and droopy. Use the bridle's cheek straps to adjust the height of the bit.

3 Buckle the throat latch, making sure that four fingers will easily fit between the strap and the pony's cheek. Check that the noseband is lying under the cheek straps. It should sit level, midway between the pony's cheekbone and the bit. Fasten the noseband snugly, but leave room for two fingers to fit underneath. Make sure the straps are securely in their keepers.

The bit sits over the pony's tongue in the space between the front and back teeth. Most bits are made of stainless steel, although the mouthpiece may be made of rubber or plastic. The reins are attached to the rings on each side of the mouthpiece, which also stop the bit from sliding through the mouth.

Martingale

Martingales

You may see a horse or pony wearing a neckstrap that has other straps running to the bridle or reins and to the girth. This is called a martingale. It is used to stop the horse throwing up its head so high that riding it is difficult. The running martingale pictured on the left divides into two straps through which each rein is threaded. A standing martingale has one strap which fastens directly to a plain cavesson noseband.

Saddles and stirrups

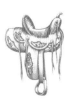

The saddle keeps you sitting securely on the pony's back in the correct position so that you can give it aids, or signals, with your legs in the right place. There are two common kinds of saddle: English and Western. It is essential that the saddle—and all tack—fit well so as not to cause the horse discomfort. A saddler is usually the best person to check this.

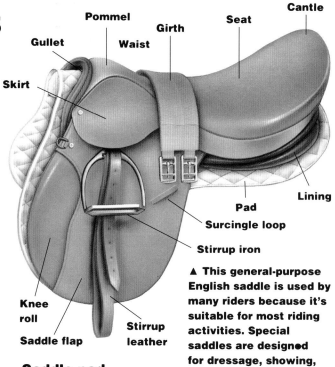

Pommel · Gullet · Waist · Girth · Seat · Cantle · Skirt · Pad · Lining · Surcingle loop · Stirrup iron · Knee roll · Saddle flap · Stirrup leather

▲ This general-purpose English saddle is used by many riders because it's suitable for most riding activities. Special saddles are designed for dressage, showing, jumping, endurance riding, and racing.

Saddle pad

The saddle pad is a cotton, sheepskin, or rubber pad which is put on under the saddle for extra comfort.

Putting on a saddle

1 Hold the saddle with your left hand on the pommel and your right hand under the seat. Standing on the near side, place the saddle gently on the highest part of the withers, then slide it down to the correct position.

2 Let down the girth, then take the girth from under the horse's belly and buckle it up beneath the saddle flaps.

3 Pull down the girth buckle guard. Run down (lower) the stirrups when you are ready to ride.

► Protective boots guard against bumps and cuts, either from the pony's other legs or if it knocks a jump.

Patterns carved into the leather for grip

High pommel, or horn, for tying on the lasso

Fender

Girth, or cinch

Snaffle bit with long cheeks, or "shanks"

Western tack

Western riding was developed from classic Spanish riding techniques by the U.S. cavalry and cowboys. The Western saddle was designed for a horse and rider spending hours or days on the range Its deep seat spread the weight of the rider and kept him secure. Wide leather flaps called fenders which protect the legs became part of the stirrup leathers.

Every saddle is built around a wooden or plastic frame called a saddletree. Its cushioned panels help to place your weight evenly, making it easier for the pony to carry you. The stirrups aren't attached to the saddle but hang from bars under the skirt. A girth made of leather, cotton, or webbing fits around the pony's belly to hold everything in place.

Cleaning tack

Leather needs regular care to keep it supple and safe to use. Ideally, tack should be cleaned after each ride. Once a week it must be taken apart and all the pieces cleaned thoroughly. Here's how to do a quick clean:

1 Wash the bit and wipe the stirrup irons with a clean damp cloth.

2 Hang the bridle on a high hook, and put the saddle on a saddle stand or over your knee.

3 Wipe the leatherwork on both sides with a damp cloth, but don't get the leather too wet.

4 Dampen the soap and rub the sponge into it, taking care not to make too much lather. Soap the leather with the sponge, then polish it with a soft dry cloth.

High hook for bridle

Lifestyles

 Given a choice, most ponies would certainly prefer to live outdoors rather than in a barn or stable. Being outside is closest to a horse's natural way of life. However, although being at grass may be a natural kind of lifestyle, there's much more to the outdoor life than letting a pony loose in the nearest field. Great care must be taken to choose a field that is both safe and suitable.

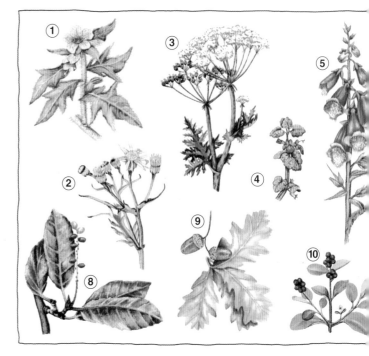

▼ Keep pasture in good condition by resting it occasionally and picking up droppings regularly.

Gate
Make sure the gate is wide, sturdy, and pony-proof. Care must be taken whenever leading a pony in or out of the field.

Fencing
Horses are amazingly accident-prone and great escape artists! Fences must be secure, safe, and in good repair. Thick hedges or post and rail are best. Any wire needs to be kept taut.

Shelter
A pony in a field cannot move to find shelter as its wild cousins can. Trees offer some protection from bad weather or hot summer sun, but ideally you should provide a special shelter.

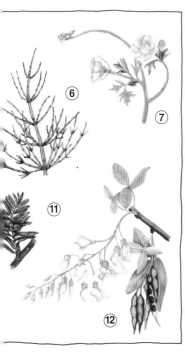

Poisonous plants

Tasty grazing contains herbs and grasses which are good for horses—but watch out for poisonous plants. Here are some common ones:

1   Henbane
2   Ragwort
3   Hemlock
4   Ground ivy
5   Foxglove
6   Horsetail
7   Buttercup
8   Laurel
9   Oak
10 Privet
11 Yew
12 Laburnum

▶ Horses kept in a barn or in stables rely on us for their every need.

Stable life

Horses weren't designed to live indoors, but many are kept that way because it's often easier for us to look after them. Ideally, every horse should go out into a field for a while each day.

Good grass

The amount of goodness in grass can vary. Pasture needs to be well-drained and neither too rich nor too sour. There should be at least 1¹/₂ acres (6,000 sq. m) of grass per pony.

Some ponies are better suited to living outdoors than others. Hardy breeds will grow thick winter coats to cope with all weathers. Finer-bred types with Arabian or Thoroughbred ancestry will need the help of a rug and extra food to keep warm in cold conditions.

Water

Every field needs a constant supply of fresh water, either piped to a trough or from a clean, free-flowing stream.

Company

Lonely ponies are unhappy ponies. Always provide a field-mate such as a donkey or, preferably, another horse.

▲ Field-kept ponies should be visited twice a day to check that they are all right.

In the stable

Looking after a stable-kept horse is a big responsibility. All stabled horses should have a large and comfortable place to live, regular work, and plenty of activity to watch to stop them from getting bored.

In the past horses were often tied up in stalls, which meant that many could be kept in a small area. Today, however, most horses and ponies have the freedom of a box stall, built of timber, stone, or bricks. Stabling is often built inside the shelter of a large barn. Deep beds of straw or wood shavings keep stabled horses warm and comfortable, but they must be kept very clean.

Yard routine

Horses love routines. A stabled pony will soon get to know when to expect a visit, so it is unkind and even harmful to change the times you arrive each day.

Daily tasks

Some jobs, such as tidying up the muck heap or disinfecting the floor of the box stall, can be done once per week, but others need to be done every day.

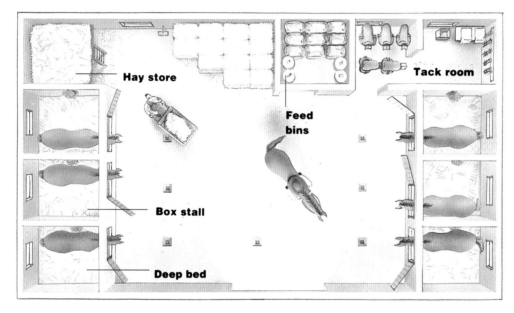

Hay store

Tack room

Feed bins

Box stall

Deep bed

The ideal stable

The minimum box stall size is 14 x 12 ft. (4.3 x 3.6m) for a horse and 12 x 10 ft. (3.6 x 3m) for a pony. The box should be 10 ft. (3m) high and the door 4 ft. (1.25m) high and 7.25 ft. (2.2m) wide. It should have good ventilation, a non-slip floor, sloping slightly for drainage, and two tie rings, one on each side, around 5 ft.(1.5m) high.

▶ **Stable-kept horses and ponies need exercising every day.**

▼ **If you own a pony, find a daily stable routine that fits in with school and stick to it.**

Quick-release knot

A special safety knot must always be used for tying up ponies. This quick-release knot can be undone in a blink in an emergency. It should always be tied to a loop of string attached to an O ring or fence, never directly to the ring or fence itself.

1 Make a loop in the lead rope and put it through the string. Twist the loop several times.

2 Loop the free end of the rope and push it through the twisted loop.

3 To tighten pull on the end of the rope attached to the halter.

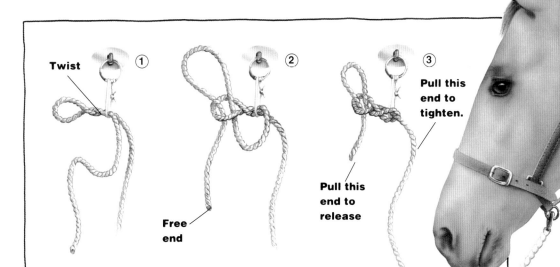

Twist

① ② ③

Pull this end to tighten.

Free end

Pull this end to release

◀ Warm New Zealand blankets are used for ponies kept outside.

Blankets

A stabled pony can't move around much to keep warm, so it needs at least one stable blanket, with extra layers on hand if it has been clipped. Modern stable blankets are usually made of quilted synthetic fabric, somewhat like a comforter, and fasten under the belly.

Clipping

During the colder months of the year horses and ponies grow thick coats and may get too hot if they are ridden regularly and if they live mainly indoors. That's why they are clipped. How much of the coat is clipped off depends on what type of work the pony has to do and how much time it spends out at grass. Most ponies don't mind being clipped, but it is a skilled job.

KEY
1 Full clip 2 Hunter clip
3 Blanket clip 4 Trace clip

① ② ③ ④

Braiding

After clipping and grooming a pony's mane and tail can be braided, especially if it's going to a show.

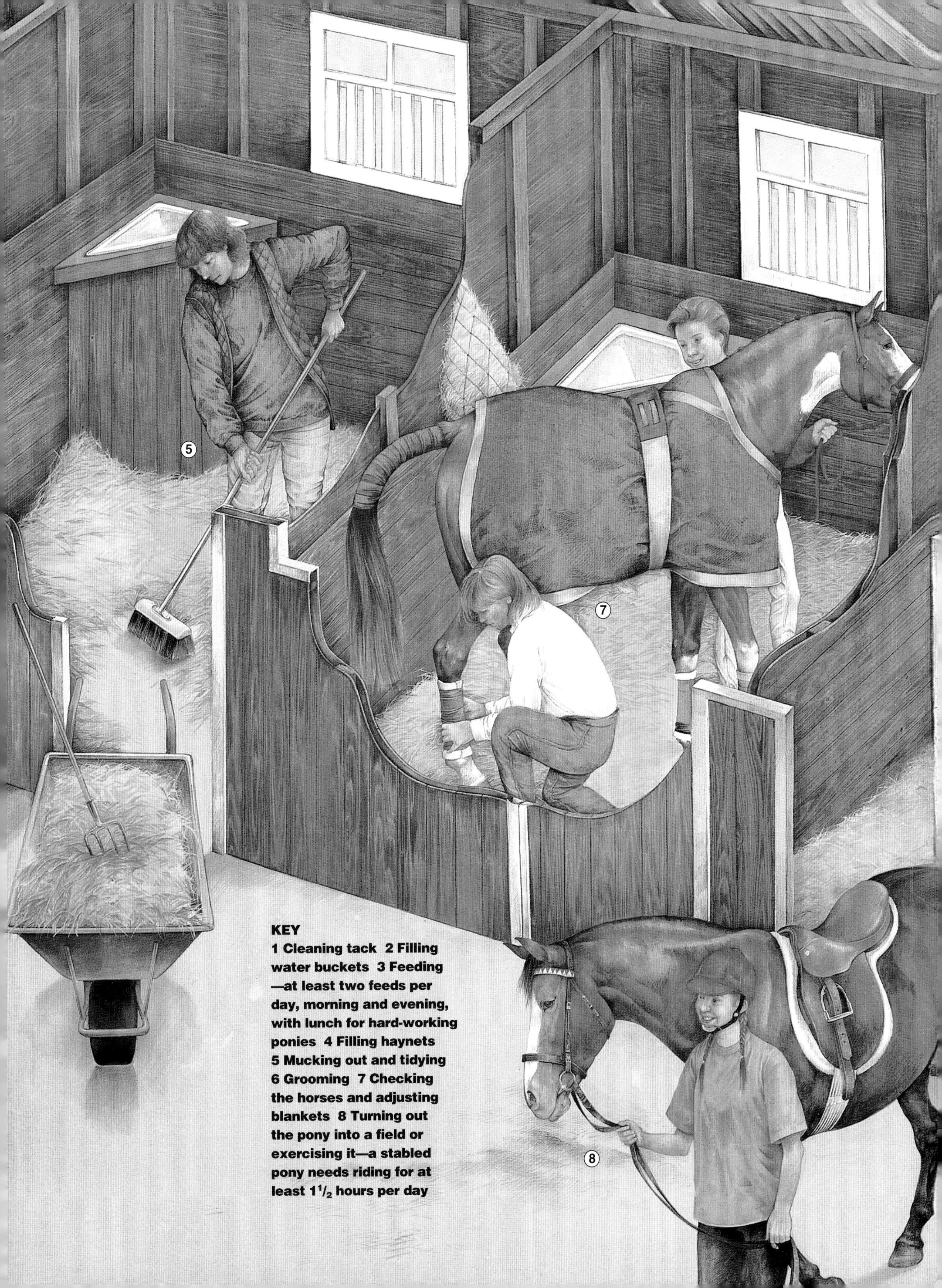

KEY
1 Cleaning tack 2 Filling
water buckets 3 Feeding
—at least two feeds per
day, morning and evening,
with lunch for hard-working
ponies 4 Filling haynets
5 Mucking out and tidying
6 Grooming 7 Checking
the horses and adjusting
blankets 8 Turning out
the pony into a field or
exercising it—a stabled
pony needs riding for at
least 1$\frac{1}{2}$ hours per day

Grooming

Grooming means more than just brushing all the mud clots off a pony to make it look neat. Regular grooming cleans the pony's skin and keeps it really healthy. If plenty of hard work is put into brushing, it will even help the blood circulation and improve the pony's muscle tone. What better way to get to know a pony than to give it a relaxing brush?

Grooming kit

1 Rubber currycomb
2 Metal currycomb
3 Plastic currycomb
Currycombs are used to help clean the body brush; also for removing caked-on dirt and mud or loose hairs. The metal currycomb must never be used on the pony.
4 Body brush
Soft brush with close-packed hairs used to clean the coat and skin deep down.
5 Dandy brush
Stiffer brush with long bristles; too hard for use on the head, mane, or tail.
6 Water brush
Similar to the dandy brush but with softer, shorter bristles. Used dampened to smooth the mane or scrub the hoofs.
7 Hoof oil and brush
Brushed onto the whole foot when dry to keep the hoofs in good condition.
8 Mane comb
For combing out knots or burrs in the mane and tail.
9 Sponges
For freshening up the pony's eyes, mouth, nostrils, and dock.
10 Sweat scraper
For wiping off excess water. Use the hard edge on the body and the flexible edge on the legs.
11 Stable cloth
Soft cloth for polishing the coat or drying wet areas.
12 Hoof pick
For removing bedding, caked mud, and stones from the hooves.

▼ Use each tool in the hand nearest the pony's head. So when grooming its near (left) side, use your left hand, and on its off (right) side, use your right hand.

Brushing tips

- Always brush in the direction the coat lies.
- Start near the head, then work along the body and down the legs.
- Use firm strokes, putting the weight of your body behind each stroke.
- Groom only when the coat is dry.
- Pick off awkward lumps of mud with your fingers.
- Fasten the halter around the neck before grooming the head so that you groom it properly.
- In cold weather leave at least one rug or blanket on when grooming to keep off the chills. Fold it back in sections as you groom.
- Most ponies love being groomed, but some have ticklish areas. Watch out for fidgeting or flicking ears which may tell you a nip or even a kick may be on the way.
- Don't forget to clean the grooming kit too!

Ponies living outside all or most of the time need their coats to be as waterproof as posssible. These ponies need only a light groom, otherwise you will remove the natural grease that keeps them warm and dry. Stable-kept ponies can be given a thorough grooming every day to add a real sparkle to their coats.

Using a hoof pick

A pony's feet need to be cleaned out twice a day to dislodge mud and stones or dirty stable bedding. The foot should be held by its front part and cleaned from heel to toe. This avoids hurting the sensitive frog (the "V"-shaped part of the sole).

▲ The hoof pick is an essential part of the grooming kit.

An individual diet

What a particular pony needs to eat depends on its size (big horses eat more than little ponies), how much it is exercised, whether it is kept in a stable or out at grass, and its age (young and old ponies have different needs). Feed more in cold weather when a lot of energy is used up keeping warm.

Food and feeding

Because every horse and pony is different, each one must be given a diet that suits its particular needs. However, whether a pony is large or small, fit or fat, its menu must be based on special feeding rules. Every horse or pony needs a diet that provides it with carbohydrates for energy and warmth, protein to build and repair its body, fats for heat and energy, fiber to help digestion, and vitamins and minerals for general good health.

◄ **Meals can be given in a manger (a trough in a stable) or in a bucket.**

KEY
1 Flaked corn—for energy and to help a pony put on weight
2 Pony pellets—balanced mixture of food pressed into cubes or pellets
3 Bran—for extra fiber
4 Coarse mix—ready-made mixture such as pellets
5 Chaff—chopped straw with added molasses for fiber

① ② ③ ④ ⑤

▲ To find out a horse's or pony's weight, you can take it to a weighbridge or measure it around the girth with a special measuring tape.

6 **Dried sugar beet—** a good source of fiber; must be soaked
7 **Salt block—to replace minerals**
8 **Rolled oats—for horses doing lots of work**
9 **Flaked barley—for energy and condition**

Feeding facts

A pony needs to eat roughly 2% of its body weight in food every day. An average 14 hh pony weighs around 770 lbs (350kg), so it'll eat about 15 lbs (7kg) of food a day. The less the pony is ridden, the more of this can be given as bulk feed (such as grass and hay) and less as concentrates (such as pony pellets).

During the warmer months grass is all that most ponies need to eat. However, when grass is poor or unavailable, they should be fed on hay. Hay is simply grass that has been cut and dried when it is at its best. Grass and hay are called bulk feeds. Although they are the main sources of fiber, which keep the digestive system working properly, they don't contain much energy. Therefore ponies should be fed other foods, such as pony pellets and cereals, whenever extra energy is needed. These foods are called concentrated feeds.

Golden rules of feeding

● Feed little and often.
● Always provide plenty of fresh water—a horse can drink up to 14 gallons (55 liters) per day.
● Allow an hour or more after feeding before you ride.
● Keep to a set routine.
● Make no sudden changes in diet.
● Feed plenty of fiber such as hay or chaff.
● Feed lots of succulents, such as carrots and apples.
● Give only the best-quality foods.
● Keep buckets and scoops clean.

Fit and healthy

Two important people help keep a well-cared-for horse or pony in the best of health— the vet and the farrier (blacksmith).

Getting to know the signs when a pony is feeling unwell helps its owner decide when to call the vet. Illness or injury aren't the only times a visit may be needed. A vet helps with routine health care, too, such as rasping (filing down) the teeth, injections, and worming.

Common illnesses

Ponies can get laminitis, a painful, crippling disease often caused by over feeding. Another common illness is colic, a kind of stomachache. Colic should be suspected if a pony avoids its food and is restless and sweaty with a high temperature (normal is about 100°F [38°C]). The vet should be called immediately.

▶ **Horses need yearly vaccinations to help stop them catching two very dangerous diseases— tetanus and equine flu. The vet can give both injections together.**

Warning: Worms

All horses and ponies carry worm parasites inside them. A pony will eat worm eggs along with grass. As the worm larvae grow, they cause the pony to lose weight or get stomachache. Dosing a horse or pony every 6–8 weeks with worming powder or paste helps to keep worms at bay.

Lameness

Horses can go lame due to an injury or an illness. A wound, heat, or swelling usually shows the vet the cause.

▲ **If a horse goes lame, trotting it up will show which leg is causing the problem, and often why. The horse is led away from the vet and back again at a walk and trot.**

Health checklist

Watching a pony carefully will soon show whether or not it is feeling well. It should have:

• ears pricking to and fro, so that it looks alert

• glossy coat lying flat

• loose and supple skin

• a good appetite

• a good thirst

• regular bowel movements

• bright eyes

• no puffiness or heat in the legs

• body filled out with good muscle tone, but not fat

• weight distributed evenly on all four feet.

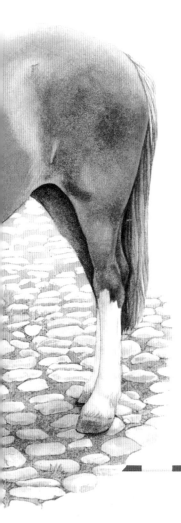

Hoof care

A pony needs to see the farrier or blacksmith every 4–6 weeks to trim back hoof growth (the horn) and replace any worn shoes with new ones.

Wall of hoof

Toe

A horse's hoofs are growing all the time, just like our fingernails. Because wild horses and ponies are always on the move over rough land, their hardy feet wear naturally into shape. Ponies living in a stable or a small field would soon grow uncomfortably long hooves, which might crack if not trimmed.

When a pony is ridden often, its hooves wear down faster than they can grow. That's why most horses and ponies wear metal shoes, especially if they are ridden on hard surfaces.

▼ This fullered shoe is used for most riding horses and ponies. It is grooved to lighten its weight and give extra grip.

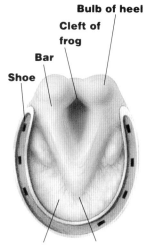

Bulb of heel

Cleft of frog

Bar

Shoe

Sole   **Point of frog**

▼ The farrier heats a steel shoe in a furnace, tries it against the pony's foot for size, then hammers it into shape for a perfect fit before nailing it on. Farriers are so skilled that shoeing doesn't hurt the pony at all.

IN THE PAST

 Long ago, by the light of flickering torches, prehistoric people drew pictures of running horses on the walls of their caves. The people were hunters, and the horses their prey.

However, as time passed, this particular source of food became

▲ Statue of an Etruscan horse and rider

instead a useful beast of burden, a precious possession, and a symbol of folklore and legend. Through the centuries, the horse has become our workmate, friend,

▲ Knight from the Isle of Lewis chess set, mid- to late-1100s

and partner, and has come to share with us a very special bond.

▶ Indian miniature painting of the Mogul emperor Shah Jahan out riding with one of his sons, 1615

◀ Cave painting at Lascaux, France, around 15,000 B.C.

Myth and magic

When Stone Age people painted horses on the walls of caves, they may have been conjuring up spirits to help them with the hunt. Since then, horses have often been used in religious rituals and even worshiped.

The first tribespeople to master the art of taming and riding the horse gained speed and power beyond their wildest dreams. It's no wonder that in people's imagination horses took on magical powers, and became part of legend and folklore across the world.

◄ Most centaurs were warlike and loved to fight.

Centaurs

The centaur of Greek mythology had the head and shoulders of a man with the lower body and legs of a horse. Centaurs were passionate and warlike and liked to drink. The most famous centaur was named Chiron. Unlike most of the others, he was wise and just. Chiron taught hunting, medicine, and music to Achilles and other famous Greek heroes. Legend says that when Chiron was killed by Hercules, Zeus, the father of the gods, honored him by placing him among the stars as the constellation Centaurus, along with another centaur, Sagittarius.

Pegasus

Pegasus was a beautiful white winged stallion. A Greek legend tells how Bellerophon tamed Pegasus with the help of the goddess Athene and how Pegasus helped him defeat a fire-breathing monster. But when Bellerophon tried to fly Pegasus to Mount Olympus, the home of the gods, Zeus sent a gadfly to sting the horse. Pegasus bucked and threw Bellerophon to Earth, flying on to Mount Olympus alone.

Odin and Sleipnir

Odin was the king and father of all the gods of Viking mythology. He was said to be the creator of the Earth, and struck fear into the hearts of gods and humans alike.

Odin had many adventures riding his fantastic white eight-legged horse, Sleipnir.

▼ **Stories tell how Sleipnir could gallop over land, sea, and air.**

▼ **The unicorn was a magical white, horselike creature with a twisted horn on its forehead. Legends say that it could be tamed only by a maiden.**

Ancient civilizations prized and respected horses above all other animals. Horses became symbols of status and wealth and the mounts of kings and warriors. So, naturally, the gods had horses, too, and ancient myths are full of tales of supernatural horses and horselike creatures. Often these horses were unruly and hard to control. Sometimes they took on strange and terrifying forms.

Horses in war

Imagine a cold, gray morning 5,000 years ago. Two desert tribes are lined up for battle, face to face, armed only with spears and axes. Suddenly, over the hill sweep the first horse-drawn chariots, carrying archers and warriors hurling spears. What a deadly surprise they must have been! The mobility horses gave to people changed the way of war forever and helped to shape history.

Armed riders have played a crucial part in warfare for centuries. It was only in World War I (1914–18) that tanks and powerful weaponry took horses out of the firing line.

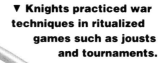

▼ Knights practiced war techniques in ritualized games such as jousts and tournaments.

► A knight's horse was called a destrier, or warhorse. It was about the size of a modern heavy hunter.

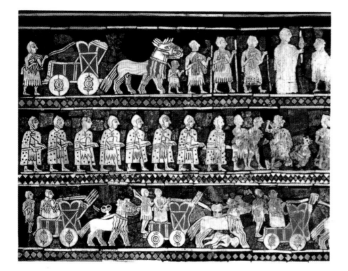

Call the cavalry!
In the Middle Ages, knights and horses wore armor in battle.

◄ Sumerian infantry and charioteers driving prisoners before them, from the Standard of Ur, *circa* 2,500 B.C.

Although the armor helped to protect them, it also slowed the horses down. By the 1700s, fast-mounted soldiers called cavalry, armed with only swords or guns, became an army's main fighting force.

Bucephalus

The greatest cavalry leader of ancient times was the Macedonian king Alexander the Great, whose armies conquered half the known world. Alexander tamed the beautiful black horse Bucephalus, which no one else dared to ride. When Bucephalus died, Alexander built a city in its honor.

◀ **Alexander on Bucephalus**

▼ **War chariots of the British queen Boudicca, whose army fought the Romans in A.D. 60**

Civil War

During the Civil War (1861–65), both sides—the Union troops and the Confederates—had cavalry in their armies. Cavalry also carried messages between camps and scouted enemy positions.

▼ **Approximately 375,000 horses were killed during World War I.**

▲ **General Ulysses S. Grant and his cavalry officers**

World War I

During World War I, tough and hardy horse breeds such as the Australian Waler were used as officers' mounts and for hauling artillery and ambulances.

Going places

For thousands of years before the days of cars, trucks, buses, and trains, transportation meant horses. Whether leading a packhorse, riding, or driving a carriage, anyone or anything going places went by horse power.

Fashion parades

In Europe, riding or leading a packhorse was often the best way to get around, right up until the early 1600s. Gradually, roads and carriage design improved, leading to the heyday of horse transportation from the late 1600s to mid-1800s. Carriages soon became a status symbol, and outings in the park were a chance for the rich to impress onlookers with their elegant, eye-catching turnouts. The spirited American Morgan and, in Britain, the high-stepping Hackney were two fashionable horse breeds much in demand for pleasure driving. Today, carriage driving competitions are held all over the world, keeping alive skills from the past.

Changing times

The building of the railroads saw the end of the stagecoach era. But for shorter riding trips it wasn't until the early 1900s that the automobile finally replaced horse-drawn transportation.

Phaeton carriage

Hansom cab

Hobby-horse

Hack

▲ **Stagecoaches drawn by teams of fast, fit horses transformed communications and made long-distance travel possible for everyone.**

▲ **In the Middle Ages, nobles and kings prided themselves on their magnificent Spanish and Arabian horses.**

Harness breeds

Horses used for pulling are called draft horses. Heavy draft refers to the biggest and strongest animals required for haulage work. Light draft horses are faster types with good endurance used for transportation and drawing carriages.

Dray

Early people probably rode horses to hunt, but in ancient civilizations horses were used mostly as beasts of burden, harnessed to carts or war chariots. Riding was a sign of rank and nobility. It became part of everyday life only during the Middle Ages after saddlery was developed.

Horse-drawn streetcar

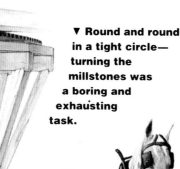

▼ Round and round in a tight circle—turning the millstones was a boring and exhausting task.

Pulling power

Until the Middle Ages, carts and plows were pulled mainly by oxen. Then, people in Europe discovered the breathtaking pulling power and intelligence of heavy horses, and for hundreds of years these placid, solid servants helped to plow the land, turn the mills, and haul farm and factory wagons.

Horsepower

The word "horsepower" is a modern-day reminder of the heavy horse's contribution to our world. Horsepower is a unit that is used to measure machine power (1 unit of horsepower = 746 watts). How else could the salesmen of the new-fangled industrial machines describe them to customers who, like generations before them, had used horses for every imaginable job that needed doing!

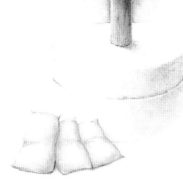

Daily grind

Donkeys, mules, and horses have been used to turn millstones to grind wheat into flour since ancient times. Later, horse-wheels or "gins" provided the power to keep early factory machines and furnaces running.

▲ The harness is a complicated arrangement of straps and buckles worn by draft horses. It enables the horse to pull its load and the driver to stay in control.

The progress made possible by the work of heavy horses helped to lay the foundations for the Industrial Revolution of the 1800s. Horse power was used to work machines and carry newly manufactured goods to ships for export. However, once steam engines were invented, the use of the heavy horse declined as its tasks were taken over by machinery.

On the land

A team of horses was as essential to the farmer of the past as a tractor is today. From the 1500s, horses were an absolute necessity for every task on the farm, from plowing and harrowing (smoothing off) the fields to grinding the grain and transporting it to market.

Horse brasses

Plowmen, carters, and brewers have always proudly decorated their horses' harnesses with beautiful ornamental brasses. Originally, these were used as lucky charms and were thought to ward off evil.

▲ Each brass had a meaning. For example, the sun meant good fortune.

▲ Some farmers are once again using heavy horses, such as the Shires on this small farm in Yorkshire, England. Some breweries, too, still use horse-drawn drays for local deliveries.

▼ A draft horse pulling a barge along a canal could pull 30 tons in weight.

Transportation in tow

Until the railroads arrived, the dependable barge horse kept the Industrial Revolution on the move. Canals became a cheap and reliable way to move raw materials such as coal, grain, and cotton to factories, and manufactured goods to the cities and towns.

HORSES TODAY

 You might think that cars, trains, and tractors leave very little need for horses in today's world. It's true that nowadays only a small number of horses are bred for the traditional jobs they have done. However, although we may not depend on horses as our ancestors did, they are still very much part of our lives, if in different ways. Today, we have the chance just to enjoy horses and ponies, to love being with

▲ Racing over huge steeplechase fences tests stamina as well as speed.

them, and to have fun riding them and developing their talents by training them for different kinds of sports.

▼ Polo is said to be the oldest and fastest team game in the world. It was invented by the Chinese over 1,500 years ago.

► In flat racing, jockeys use short stirrups to redistribute their weight and to help the horses gallop at their best.

On the beat

In cities as far apart as London, New York, Tokyo, and Sydney, police horses can be seen patrolling the streets.

▼ New York policewoman and her horse.

These unflappable, superbly-trained horses give their riders a high viewpoint and the ability to move quickly in any direction—perfect for crowd control. Just a few of a police horse's other tasks include traffic duty, searching for missing people in a crowd, or simply hoofing the beat.

Working horses

In many countries, donkeys, mules, and horses still carry on their traditional roles of providing transportation and a livelihood for their owners, as they have done for thousands of years.

All around the world, horses can still be found helping with tasks where machines cannot match their unique talents— from pulling tourist carriages in cities to rounding up cattle on a ranch or leading a big parade.

Cowboy horses

In cattle-raising countries, cowhands have special names and ride special horses. North American cowboys usually ride a Quarter Horse, named after its amazing speed in a quarter-mile race. Mexican vaqueros work on fiery mustangs, while Argentinian gauchos ride the Criollo. Australian stockmen use mainly Walers—hardy horses bred by early settlers.

Donkey work

Sure-footed on the steepest mountainside and tough enough to keep going all day, donkeys and mules still work hard earning their living in countries such as Greece, Spain, and Morocco.

◄ **This Moroccan donkey will carry its owner and several baskets of produce to market and back.**

▼ **The gaucho's lightning-quick horse works almost on instinct, picking out a calf from the herd. Once the calf is lassoed, the horse stops dead and throws its weight against the rope to hold it still.**

▼ **In many snowy north European countries, sturdy ponies pull sleighs carrying passengers, fuel, or food.**

The entertainers

Horses are natural entertainers. Even an old pony turned loose in a field will show off with a kick and buck to a passing audience, and a star performer of the circus ring or sports arena certainly knows it's special every time the crowd bursts into applause. Horses have topped the bill ever since the days of the spectacular chariot races in ancient Rome. Today, their grace, strength, and skill can still make us gasp whenever they step into the spotlight.

▼ The drum horse of Britain's Household Cavalry carries a huge pair of solid silver drums. The drummer steers by reins attached to the stirrups, but the horse never puts a foot wrong.

Ride 'em, cowboy!

Rodeos began in the late 1800s in the cattle lands of North America. Today, professional cowboys keep traditional rodeo skills alive.

Circus horses

Animals are used less in circuses now, but once the flowing manes and tails of the swirling liberty horses were among the most breathtaking sights of the Big Top.

▶ *The Circus*, by Georges Seurat, 1891.

Pure poetry

The white horses of Vienna's Spanish Riding School are famous all over the world. The school is the oldest of several riding academies founded in the 1500s. It uses only Spanish horses, which for 400 years have been bred at Lipizza. Lipizzaner horses and riders take many years to train. Only the most gifted become the top haute école (high school) performers.

▲ Today's big rodeos have been called the greatest outdoor shows on Earth. Events include bronco riding, calf roping, steer wrestling, and wagon racing.

A bronco rider has to try to stay on the back of a wildly bucking horse for at least 8 seconds—sometimes without a saddle!

53

Young riders

1 When you are with ponies, it doesn't matter how young you are or even if you have only recently begun riding—you can still have a lot of fun! A riding vacation, helping out at the stables after a lesson, or joining the Pony Club (a worldwide organization for young riders) are great ways to learn more about riding and pony care. And when you're feeling brave, there's the excitement of your first show.

Clear round

If you and your pony enjoy jumping there's sure to be a class to enter at a local show. Beginner riders can try the smaller jumps.

▲ **Jumping a natural fence at a working hunter show class.**

In other classes, ponies and riders of the same size or age and experience compete.

At a show

There's something for everyone at a show. Horses and ponies that are especially handsome and obedient can take part in ridden showing classes ("under saddle") according to their type. Youngsters or purebred ponies can be shown off on a lead-rein (called "in-hand"). In equitation classes, which judge a rider's ability, ordinary four-legged friends can be winners, too!

◄ **Even the tiniest rider on a lead-rein pony can take part in a small show.**

Vaulting

Vaulting, or "voltige," is like gymnastics on horseback. A single vaulter or a team has to make daring leaps and balance on a horse that is cantering steadily on a lunge.

Perhaps your dream is to become a top showjumping or dressage rider one day. It may seem a daunting task, but don't forget—all famous riders started out by taking their pony to local shows and pony club games.

Handicapped riding

All over the world, there are groups to help everyone who would like to try riding. Through organizations such as North American Riding for the Handicapped, riders can do things like take lessons or participate in local shows, or even in international competitions.

Ready, get set, go!

Pony club games are like some of the races at a school sports day. The only difference if that the contestants are on horseback. Games include flag races, sack races, apple bobbing, and bending (racing in and out of a line of poles).

▼ Races at pony club games are fast and furious.

International sport

Today's competition horses are bred to be the very best at their particular sport—to gallop faster, jump higher, or move with more grace and power than their rivals. Equestrian sports are different from any other sports. Two participants are involved, and both horse and rider must be talented and fit. A winning partnership means years of hard work and training, and to reach the top takes special teamwork.

Harness racing

Harness racing is popular in the United States and Russia, where breeds such as the American Standardbred and the Orlov Trotter have been developed especially for the sport.

▼ Some harness races are for pacing horses, which trot using the pair of legs on the same side rather than those diagonally opposite.

▼ The cross-country course at a three-day event usually provides plenty of thrills and spills.

Eventing

Eventing, or horse trials, is an all-around test of a horse's and rider's fitness and skill. The competition has three phases—dressage, cross-country, and show jumping. At the highest level it takes place over three days.

Show jumping

Show jumping has the same basic rules for a novice class at a local show and an international championship. The horse and rider must jump a course of colored fences without picking up any faults from knocking one over or refusing. Riders with equal faults go again in a "jump off," which may be timed, to decide the winner.

Dressage

"Dressage" means training. It aims to show the horse and rider in perfect harmony. Each pair performs a test of set exercises which are judged and awarded marks out of ten.

▲ Endurance races can cover up to 93 miles (150 km) in one or two days, often over difficult ground. Riders may dismount during a race to rest their horses, which must pass strict checks by a vet.

Most event horses are Thoroughbreds, which have the combination of speed, boldness, stamina, good movement, and big jump needed for this tough sport. Showjumpers need power and agility, while dressage horses must be supple and balanced with lovely paces.

Horse breeds

Today, there are over 200 recognized breeds of horses and ponies. Breeds are groups of horses that have been bred to obtain particular features, such as a particular color, height, action, and conformation. All these features are clearly defined, often by a breed society, which keeps a special list, or Stud Book, of horses belonging to that breed.

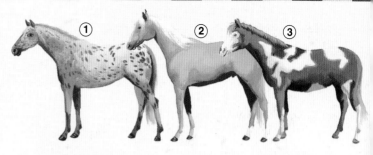

Horse colors

Certain colors of horse and pony are recognized as breeds in the United States, although in the rest of the word they are considered to be types (see below left).

NAME	HEIGHT	COLOR
1 Appaloosa	14–15.2 hh	Spots unique to each horse; basic patterns include blanket, marble, leopard, and snowflake
2 Palomino	varies	Golden with light mane and tail
3 Pinto	14–15.2 hh	Irregular patches of white and black or brown

Horse types

As well as breeds, there are also types. Instead of belonging to a breed with a Stud Book or pedigree, a type is produced by crossing other breeds to get a horse or pony suited to a particular purpose. The best known include the cob, hack, hunter, polo pony, and riding pony. Most polo ponies are crosses between small Thoroughbreds and other breeds, such as the Argentinian Criollo. Despite usually being over 14.2 hh, they are always called ponies.

Riding ponies are suitable for young riders. They are usually cross-bred from Thoroughbreds or Arabians and native ponies.

◄ Riding pony

Ponies

All horses under 14.2 hh are called ponies. Pony breeds are strong and hardy with short-striding paces. Most ponies are quick-witted and full of character.

NAME	HEIGHT	COLOR
4 Exmoor	11.2–12.2 hh	Bay, brown, dun
5 Welsh	Up to 13.2 hh	Any solid color
6 Highland	12.2–14.2 hh	Usually gray, dun, brown, or black; sometimes bay or liver chestnut
7 Dales	13.2–14.2 hh	Mainly black or brown
8 New Forest	12–14 hh	Any solid color
9 Connemara	13–14.2 hh	Mainly gray; also bay, brown, black, or dun
10 Fjord	13–14.2 hh	Pale dun
11 Fell	13–14 hh	Bay, brown, black, or gray
12 Dartmoor	Up to 12.2 hh	Any solid color
13 Haflinger	13–14.2 hh	Palomino or chestnut with blond mane and tail
14 Shetland	Up to 42 in	Any color
15 Riding pony	Up to 14.2 hh	Any color

Little horses

A few pony breeds have features usually seen in horses rather than in ponies but at a much smaller scale.

NAME	HEIGHT	COLOR
16 Icelandic	12–14 hh	Any color
17 Falabella	Up to 34 in	Any color
18 Caspian	10–12.1 hh	Bay, chestnut, or gray

Sports horses

Sports horses are either hot bloods or warm bloods. Arabians and Thorough-breds are hot bloods. Warm-blood breeds come from crossing hot bloods and warm bloods.

NAME	HEIGHT	COLOR
24 Arabian	14–15 hh	Gray, bay, chestnut, or black
25 Lipizzaner	15–16.1 hh	Usually gray, sometimes bay
26 Thoroughbred	14.2–17 hh	Most solid colors
27 Cleveland Bay	16–16.2 hh	Bay or brown
28 Barb	14–15 hh	Bay, brown, black, chestnut, or gray
29 Andalucian	15.1–15.3 hh	Usually gray, also bay, black, chestnut, or roan
30 Hackney	14–15.3 hh (horse) Under 14 hh (pony)	Bay, brown, chestnut, black
31 Selle Français	15–17 hh	Mostly chestnut, bay, or brown
32 Waler	14.2–16 hh	Any solid color
33 Quarter Horse	14.1–16 hh	Most colors
34 Akhal-Teke	14.2–15.2 hh	Bay, gray, black, or dun with metallic sheen
35 Saddlebred	15–16 hh	Bay, black, gray, or chestnut
36 Morgan	14–15.2 hh	Bay, black, or chestnut
37 Standardbred	14–16.1 hh	Bay, brown, black, or chestnut
38 Trakehner	16–16.2 hh	Any solid color

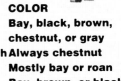

Heavy horses

Today, most heavy horses are used for displays and shows rather than as workhorses.

NAME	HEIGHT	COLOR
19 Shire	16–18 hh	Bay, black, brown, chestnut, or gray
20 Suffolk Punch	15.3–16.1 hh	Always chestnut
21 Ardennais	15–16 hh	Mostly bay or roan
22 Clydesdale	16–17 hh	Bay, brown, or black with white legs and face
23 Percheron	14.3–16 hh (Postier) or 16–17.3 hh	Usually gray, also black and roan

59

Glossary

action How a horse moves.

aged A horse over seven years old.

aid Signals a rider uses to communicate with a horse. Natural aids are the hands, seat, legs, and voice. Artificial aids include whips, spurs, and **martingales**.

barn sour Term used to describe a stubborn horse that won't go forward or hangs back toward its stable or friends.

bars The parts of the gums at the sides of the mouth where there are no teeth and where the **bit** lies.

bit The part of the **bridle** that goes in the horse's mouth to give the rider more control.

bit converter A pair of short, round leather straps that buckle to the snaffle and curb rings on a **Pelham** bit so that a single rein can be used.

box stall An individual stable.

breastplate/breast collar A strap that goes around the horse's neck and fastens to the front of the saddle and between the forelegs to the **girth**. It stops the saddle from slipping backward, especially when galloping.

bridle The combination of straps that fit around a horse's head and are used to control it for riding.

bridoon A bit resembling a **snaffle** that is used with a curb and reined independently of it.

brood mare Mare kept just for breeding.

brushing A type of bad **action** in which the lower legs move so closely

MARE AND FOAL

that they strike into each other.

cast When a horse lies down and is unable to get up.

chaff Straw, or a mixture of hay and straw, chopped into short lengths and added to the feed to provide more fiber.

clear round Completing a course of jumps without any penalties.

clip 1) Shearing off the winter coat to stop a horse from sweating too much when worked. 2) Part of a horseshoe that turns over the edge of the foot to help keep the shoe in place.

colic A kind of stomachache that horses get, often caused by bad feeding.

colt A young male horse under three years of age.

conformation The shape of a horse or the way it is put together.

crupper A broad strap that is fixed to the back of the saddle going around a pony's tail to stop the saddle from slipping back too far.

dam The mother of a foal.

dished face A face that has a concave profile, as in an Arabian horse

dishing A poor **action** in which the front feet are thrown out to the sides.

double bridle A **bridle** with two **bits**; used on highly trained horses for **dressage** and showing.

dressage An elegant equestrian sport in which horses are trained to be very obedient to their riders and perform a set of special movements.

ergot Hard lump that can be felt at the back of the fetlock joint.

farrier A person who shoes horses.

feather Long hair growing on the lower legs, especially in heavy breeds like the Shire and Clydesdale.

filly A young female horse

BRIDLE — **Headstall** — **Reins** — **Browband** — **Throat latch** — **Cheek strap** — **Noseband** — **Bit**

under three years of age.

flehmen An odd, lip-curling expression made by horses and ponies when they smell or taste something interesting or by a stallion interested in a mare.

foal A baby horse.

forehand The half of the horse in front of the saddle (see hindquarters).

forelock Section of mane that falls forward between the ears.

frog Rubbery, V-shaped structure in the center of the sole under the hoof.

gall A sore around the belly caused by a **girth** that is dirty or too tight.

gelding A castrated male horse.

gestation The length of time a fetus is in the womb before being born. In horses this is 11 months.

girth A broad strap placed around the horses's belly to keep the saddle on. In Western riding called a cinch.

going The condition of the ground for riding on—wet ground is soft going, and very dry ground is hard going.

green Term applied to a young, inexperienced horse.

gymkhana A small show with games and races for ponies and their riders.

hackamore A type of **bridle** that does not use a bit.

halter A simple piece of headgear, often made of rope, for leading and tying up; may include a noseband, headstall, and **throat latch**.

hand Unit of measurement of a horse's height. One hand equals approximately 4 in. (10cm).

hindquarters The half of the body behind the saddle area (see forehand).

hogged mane Describes a mane that has been shaved off. Hogging is done to improve the appearance of horses with short, thick necks and coarse manes.

keepers The small leather loops used to hold the spare ends of the **bridle** straps neatly in place. In Western riding called stoppers.

knee rolls Pads at the front of the flaps on an English-style saddle that help keep the rider's legs in the correct position.

laminitis A painful disease that makes a horse's feet very tender—usually caused by over eating.

latigo On a Western saddle a long strap used to do up the cinch.

leading leg The foreleg that stretches farthest forward in the canter.

liberty horse A circus horse that performs in groups without a rider.

loading Putting a horse or pony into a trailer.

lunge A long rein that is attached to a special **halter** called a lunging cavesson. The trainer sends the horse around in a circle, using a lunging whip to keep it going forward.

manège An enclosed outdoor riding arena that usually has a surface that is good in all weather.

manger A trough in a stable used for a horse's feed.

mare An adult female horse.

martingale Neckstrap attached between the forelegs to the **girth** and also the **reins** or noseband to give the rider extra control.

HALTER

near side The lefthand side of a horse (see off side)

neckstrap A strap around a pony's neck that a beginner rider can hold onto for safety. Also part of a **martingale** or **breastplate**.

New Zealand blanket A tough rug for outdoor use in the winter.

novice A beginner rider or inexperienced horse.

numnah A cotton or fleece pad used under the saddle to absorb sweat and ease pressure.

off side The righthand side of a horse (see near side).

over reaching When a hind hoof hits the heel of a foreleg, causing injury.

pastern The area of the leg between the hoof and the fetlock.

Pelham Type of **bit** used with two **reins** and a curb chain; stronger than a **snaffle**.

picking out Cleaning out the hooves.

points 1) Parts of a horse. 2) The extremities of a horse, such as the muzzle, tips of the ears, and lower legs, which are sometimes of a darker color than the rest of the body.

pulling a mane/tail Taking out hairs, a few at a time, to neaten the mane or tail.

rein 1) The long straps attached to the **bit** by a rider to control a pony. 2) The direction a rider is going around an arena—being either on the left rein or the right rein.

roller A wide strap used around the belly to keep a blanket in place.

Roman nose A convex profile, most often seen in heavy horses.

saddletree The frame around which a saddle is built.

schooling Training a horse.

shying A sudden movement sideways after taking a fright.

sire The father of a foal.

snaffle Largest family of **bits**, with one ring to each side of the mouthpiece.

sound A healthy horse that has no breathing or lameness problems.

surcingle A narrow strap used around the belly to fasten a blanket or over the saddle for extra security when galloping and jumping.

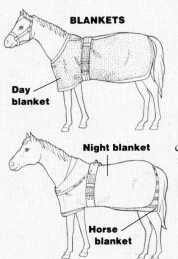

BLANKETS

Day blanket

Night blanket

Horse blanket

tack All the items of saddlery used for riding.

tendons Tough tissue that connects muscles to bones. In horses the main tendons run down the back of the cannon bones in the legs.

throat latch The strap on a **bridle** that goes under a horse's throat.

transition Changing from one pace to another.

turning out Letting a pony loose into a field.

turnout The appearance of a horse and rider.

vice A bad or nervous habit. Stable vices often start because a horse is bored. These include weaving, in which a horse sways back and forth, crib biting, and wind sucking, in which it arches its back and sucks in air. Vices shown in riding include rearing, napping (see **barn sour**), and bucking.

wind A horse's breathing.

withers The top of the shoulder blade, which forms a bony ridge at the base of the neck. Horses and ponies are measured from the ground to the highest point of the withers.

working hunter show A competition in which horses are judged according to their pace, manner, and jumping, without regard to their competition.

yearling A one-year-old horse.

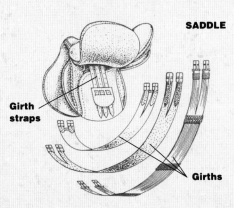

SADDLE

Girth straps

Girths

Index

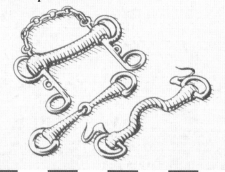

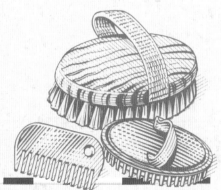

Acknowledgments

The publishers would like to thank the following
illustrators for their contribution to this book:

John Butler 6–7; **Peter Dennis** (Linda Rogers Associates) 38–43, 44–45*b*, 48–49,
52–53; **Angelika Elsbach** 30*bl*; **Lindsay Graham** (Linden Artists) 10–11, 22*bl*, 23,
32–33, 36–37, 56–57; **Ian Jackson** 8–9, 14–15, 34*l*, 35*tl*, 50–51, 54–55; **Eddy
Krähenbühl** 16–17; **Ruth Lindsay** 17*r*, 21*b*, 27*br*, 30*c*, 34–35*bc*, 35*br*; **Nicki Palin**
18–19, 26–31, 44–45*t*; **Eric Robson** (Garden Studios) 4–5, 24–25; **Eric Rowe**
(Linden Artists) 12–13; **Richard Ward** 5*r*, 6*bl*, 19*tr*, 20*bl*, 22*tr*, 27*c*, 30*t*, 32*tl*, 33*br*,
37*t*; **Wendy Webb** 20*tl* and *br*, 21*t*; **Steve Weston** (Linden Artists) 11*r*; **Andrew
Wheatcroft** (Virgil Pomfret Agency) 58–59 **Dan Wright** 46–47

Woodcuts by Peter Cornwell
Border by Julian Baker

The publishers would also like to thank the following
for supplying photographs for this book:

Page 11 Robert Harding Picture Library; 14 The Granger Collection, New York;
24 ZEFA; 36 Robert Harding Picture Library; 39, 42 Michael Holford;
43 Bridgeman Art Library/Library of Congress; 45 Bibliothèque Nationale;
48 Kit Houghton; 51 ZEFA/Damm;
54 Robert Harding Picture Library; 55, 57 Kit Houghton

Additional Consultants:
Marsha George, Longhorn Western Riding Ltd., Wiltshire, England
Lesley Ward, editor of *Young Rider* magazine, Williamsburg, Virginia

For the address of a pony club near you, write to:
Pony Clubs, Ms. Heacock, 4071 Iron Work Pike,
Lexington, KY 40511

For information on disabled riding, contact:
North American Riding for the Handicapped (N.A.R.H.)
P.O. Box 33150, Denver, CO 80233
or call 1-800-369-RIDE